This book is to be returned on or before the last date below.

Scientists and Writers

Tony D. Triggs

Wayland

Titles in the series

Country Life

Exploration

Kings and Queens

Religion

Scientists and Writers

Town Life

Cover illustrations: *Background* Swan Theatre, 1596;
inset William Shakespeare

First published in 1993 by Wayland (Publishers) Ltd
61 Western Road, Hove, East Sussex BN3 1JD

Editor: Cath Senker
Designer: John Christopher
Consultant: Linda Goddard, Primary History Advisory Teacher,
Runnymede Staff Development Centre, Surrey

British Library Cataloguing in Publication Data
Triggs, Tony D.
  Scientists and Writers. – (Tudors and Stuarts series)
  I. Title II. Series
  942.05

ISBN 0-7502-0750-7

Typeset by Strong Silent Type
Printed and bound by B.P.C.C. Paulton Books, Great Britain

Picture acknowledgements
Bodleian Library 6 (MS Ashmole 399 Fol 19r and MS Ashmole 399
Fol 22r); Edinburgh University 10; Eye Ubiquitous 5 (below),27; Guildhall
Library 17 (right); Hulton-Deutsch Collection 4,21; The Master and
Fellows, Magdalene College, Cambridge 14 (above),22 (above); Mansell
Collection 8,23; Mary Evans Picture Library 17 (left); Museum of London
(A. Fulgoni Photography) 11 (below), 13 (below); National Portrait
Gallery 12,18,22; Oxford Picture Library 16; Ann Ronan Picture Library
9 (both); Science Museum 26 (both); Thomas Photos, Oxford 24 (left);
Topham 7 (both),20,25; Wayland *cover* (both), *title page*, 11 (above),14
(below); Wellcome Institute Library 5 above),19; G Wheeler 13 (above).

Notes for teachers

Scientists and Writers draws on a wide range of exciting sources including contemporary maps, artefacts, paintings and drawings.

This book:

◆ explains some of the ideas scientists held about the human body, and shows how they discovered new ideas.

◆ shows how the theatre developed from plays performed outside in the street to performances in specially-built theatres.

◆ helps the reader to understand how we use clues from the past to learn about how people lived then.

Contents

Early medicine

The Tudor kings and queens ruled England and Wales from 1485 to 1603, and the Stuarts ruled England, Scotland and Wales from 1603 to 1714.

During this time Britain grew powerful, trading with many other countries and becoming very wealthy. Scientists made many discoveries and writers described the changing world around them.

Scholars began to do experiments to find out how the human body worked, but most people stuck to old-fashioned ideas about illnesses and how to cure them.

In Tudor and Stuart times people thought that having too much blood in their bodies made them ill. When they were sick, they tried to get rid of the extra blood to make themselves better.

Using leeches
Leeches are worm-like creatures that live in streams. They can fix themselves on to people's skin and suck their blood. The woman in the picture has some leeches on her legs. She may be ill or she may be collecting the leeches for a sick friend.

This woman's legs are covered with leeches.

Cupping glasses

Cupping glasses were small jars or pots. People warmed them up, then put them over a cut or a sore. As the cups cooled down they sucked some blood or poison from the person's body.

These diagrams show a man using cupping glasses.

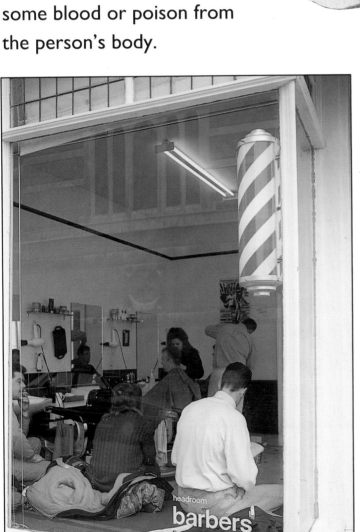

Is there a barber's shop in your town that has a red and white pole?

Barbers

Sometimes, sick people thought they should lose a lot of blood, so they went to a barber (a man who pulled out teeth, cut hair and bled the sick). The barber made a cut in their arm; he let it bleed and then he bandaged it up.

Few people could read, so shops and businesses put up signs to show what they sold or what they did. Barbers put up a striped pole like the one in the picture. It was meant to show a person's arm. Why do you think it has red and white stripes?

Modern barbers do not bleed people, and nor do doctors. Why do you think bleeding is no longer used to try to cure sick people?

Old books, old ideas

In early Tudor times doctors did not know very much about what the human body was like inside, and how it worked. Their ideas came from very old books, which people had copied out by hand and passed on to each other for hundreds of years.

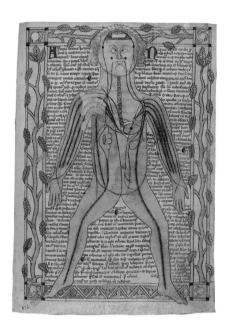

These drawings come from a thirteenth-century book about the body.

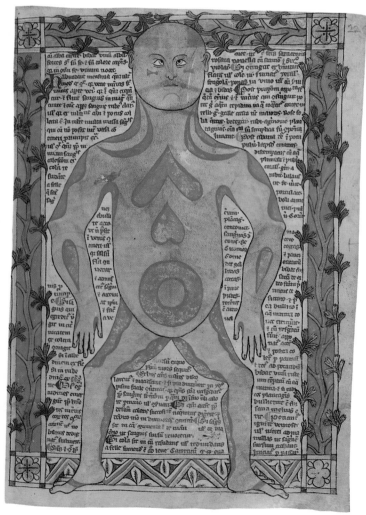

Early ideas about the body

The thirteenth-century drawing of the human body above contains a big mistake. It shows each leg with a single blood pipe. Nowadays we know there are two main blood pipes in each leg.

The drawing on the left shows the lungs, heart and stomach, but they are not quite the right shape and they are not in exactly the right place.

Old ideas about chemistry

Tudor people believed that gold could be made from other metals. The page below comes from a fifteenth-century book of instructions – which never worked!

People trying to make gold from other metals.

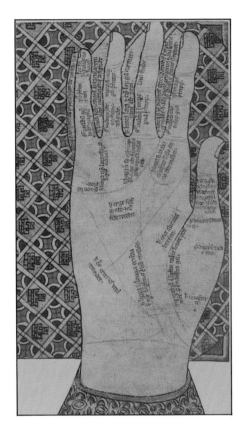

(Right) The lines on a hand. Do you think they have any meaning?

Fortune telling

Some people studied the lines on their hands. They believed that the lines showed what would happen later on in their lives.

Even today, some people try to work out the future by looking at the stars, the lines on their hands or the tea leaves left in their cups. Why do you think this sort of thing was more popular in Tudor times than it is today?

Printers at work

Printers working at a printing press in the early sixteenth century.

From the 1520s new printing machines made it easier to produce books. Some printed books contained old ideas, but many contained new ones. Some of the most important new ideas were about the human body and how it worked.

In Tudor times the Christian Church was very powerful. Its leaders were afraid that ordinary people might learn new ideas and start to question its power. The Church tried to make people stick to old ideas, but the new printed books helped them to find things out for themselves.

Andreas Vesalius

In the 1530s a man called Andreas
Vesalius (who came from Belgium but
worked in Italy) decided to do some
experiments to find out how the human
body worked. He cut up dead bodies to
see what they were like inside. Then
he drew and described the muscles
and organs he found.

(Above) A page from a book about the human
body by Andreas Vesalius. It came out in 1543.
What is Vesalius doing in the picture?

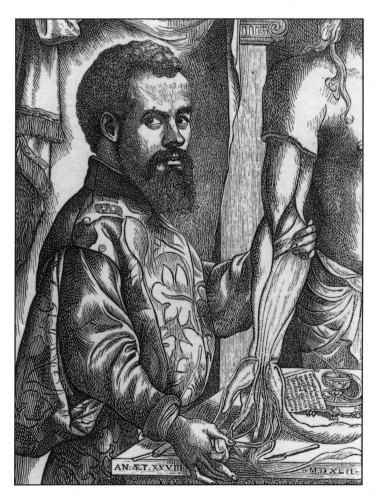

This is an engraving of Vesalius. What is he doing?

Vesalius was a teacher. When he opened
dead bodies he let his students watch.
But it was mainly the book he wrote
about the human body that spread
his ideas.

Plays and theatres

In Tudor and Stuart times plays were very popular. The main way to learn Bible stories was to watch them being acted out in the street. Other plays – some of them rude – were performed at inns and in theatres.

Men and boys decorated wagons like this one and performed plays on them.

A pageant

In large towns a set of religious plays was performed every year. Each play had its own group of actors, who did ordinary jobs for the rest of the year. For example, the bakers might act in one of the plays and the butchers in another.

Each group of actors had a wagon or cart, called a pageant. The actors used to move round the town, performing their plays in every district. In Tudor times women never acted in plays, as most people felt that this was wrong. Boys acted all the women's parts.

From courtyard to theatre

Many inns had a courtyard (a large square space with buildings all around it). Some men and boys spent their whole lives going from town to town and performing their plays in the courtyards of inns. Some members of the audience watched from the windows; others stood in the courtyard itself.

In Tudor times special theatres were built. Theatre builders copied inns by making a ring of buildings round a courtyard. One of the buildings had an archway with a stage. Part of the stage was through the archway but part of it stuck out into the courtyard. Performances in streets and inns became less common as more and more special theatres were built.

The Swan Theatre in 1596.

The remains of the Rose Theatre, which was dug up in 1989.

Artists did drawings which show us what the theatres were like, and remains discovered in the ground give us more information. The photograph on the left shows the remains of a theatre called the Rose. The theatre was dug up by archaeologists in 1989. In the time of Queen Elizabeth I (1558–1603) it was one of London's best-known theatres.

William Shakespeare

William Shakespeare lived from 1564 to 1616. He helped to run theatres and he wrote some very exciting plays, which are still performed in theatres today.

Shakespeare, Shagspere or Shaxpere?

In Shakespeare's time there were no strict rules about how to spell. Printers changed the length of words according to how much space there was on each line. Shakespeare wrote his name in several different ways. The only thing that stayed the same was the kind of pen he had to use. It was made from a feather and he had to keep dipping it in ink to write.

A famous painting of Shakespeare.

A scene from Shakespeare's play *Othello*, performed in the twentieth century.

The Rose Theatre as it was

Many of Shakespeare's plays were performed in the Rose Theatre. A modern artist drew the picture below using clues from remains in the ground and clues in old drawings. Try to imagine the scene from *Othello* (left) being acted on the stage of the Rose.

The flag was raised to tell people when a performance was about to start.

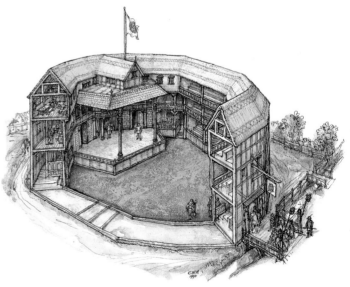

The Rose Theatre, as it was in Shakespeare's time.

A black hero

Shakespeare's play *Othello* was especially interesting to theatre audiences because the main character was usually played by a black person. Merchants had brought black people to England to work as servants and maids, but it was unusual to see a black character in a play.

Exploration and science

Tudor and Stuart explorers discovered many new lands. To do this they had to sail across stormy seas, and some lost their ships – and their lives. Shipbuilders learned to make ships larger, faster and safer, and scientists learned to make instruments such as compasses to help sailors to find their way at sea.

Learning from fish about how to build ships.

This compass was used by sailors in the seventeenth century.

Designed for speed

Nowadays we know how important it is for cars, trains and aircraft to have a smooth shape to help them slip through the air smoothly and quickly.

Ships must also have a streamlined shape to slip through water easily. In Stuart times people were learning how important this is. Fish slip through water easily, so the shipbuilders tried to copy the shape of a fish. You can see this in the drawing above.

Raleigh was interested in science (finding things out by experiment). One day he told a friend that he knew how to weigh his smoke. First he weighed his tobacco; then he smoked it and weighed the ash that was left in his pipe. The ash weighed less than the tobacco had done, so some of it must have gone up in smoke. Raleigh did a simple take-away sum to find out how much the smoke weighed.

Weighing smoke

Sir Walter Raleigh (1564 –1618) was one of the most famous explorers of Tudor and Stuart times. He found that people in America smoked tobacco leaves. No one in Britain had heard of smoking, so he brought back some tobacco for his friends.

This is the sort of sum Raleigh did:

" Weight of tobacco = 2 ounces
Weight of ash = 1 ounce
So: weight of smoke = 1 ounce "

1520s
New printing machines are developed.

1543
Andreas Vesalius publishes his book about the human body.

1580s–1610s
Sir Walter Raleigh makes voyages to America.

1590–1616
William Shakespeare writes his plays.

King James the author

James I (who ruled from 1603–1625) was a very clever man who wrote several famous books. He enjoyed writing about religion and politics. Some of the things James wrote in his books seem rather strange today.

James said in his writings that kings were like God because they had total power over people's lives. He thought that kings should be obeyed without question. James also wrote about his fear of witches.

Many scholars of the time admired James' books and Wadham College, part of Oxford University, was built with a statue of James over one of the doors.

This statue of King James I is at Oxford University.

King James I wrote about other subjects too. He wrote a book called *A Counterblast to Tobacco*. A counterblast is a fierce reply, and the book gave an answer to people who said that smoking was good for them. James thought that smoking was very harmful – and modern doctors agree with James!

(Right) The title page of King James' *Works*, a book of his writings.

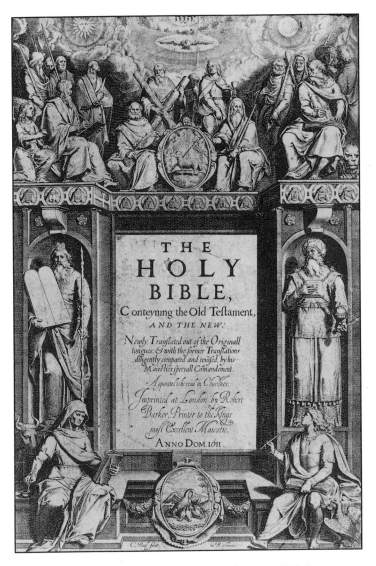

A page from the famous King James Bible, which was published in 1611.

The King James Bible

James asked a team of scholars to translate the Bible from Hebrew and Greek into English. They did their work extremely well, and their version of the Bible is very famous. We sometimes call it the King James Bible. The language seems old-fashioned today, but many people think it is very beautiful.

William Harvey

After King James' death in 1625 his son Charles became king. He became known as Charles I. Charles' doctor was a clever man called William Harvey (1578–1657), who found out about the human body by doing experiments.

The circulation of the blood

Look again at the picture at the top of page 6. It shows a single blood pipe in each leg because scientists in Tudor times believed that a single pipe could carry the blood in both directions – first down the leg and then up it again.

Harvey proved that blood can only go one way through the pipes in our bodies. He showed that there are arteries carrying blood away from the heart and veins to take it back again.

A portrait of William Harvey.

The valves in veins

The drawings below show one of Harvey's experiments. He slid his finger along someone's arm to squeeze the blood out of part of a vein. He kept his finger at one end of the empty part and it stayed empty; blood could not come into it from the other end to fill it again. This was because there were valves (special 'doors') in the vein that would only let the blood go through in one direction – towards the heart.

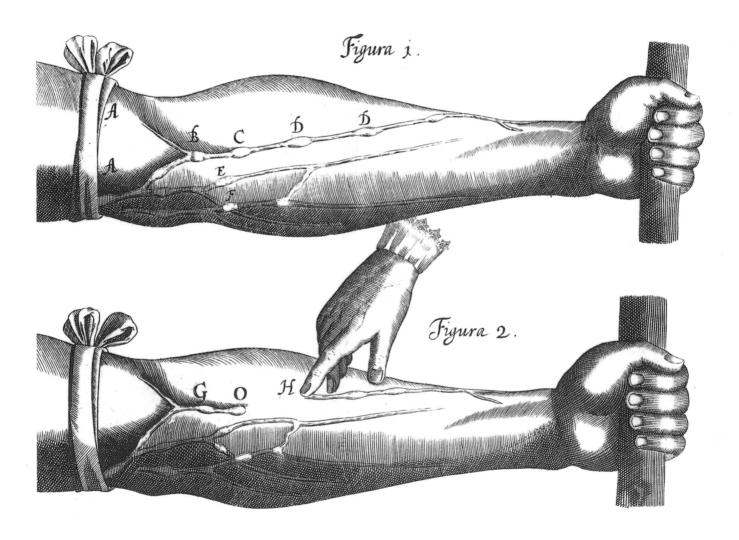

These pictures from one of Harvey's books show that there are valves in the vein of an arm.

The Restoration – and new theatres

King Charles I shared his father's idea that kings and queens should rule as they liked, and this made him very unpopular. His enemies put him in prison and a man called Oliver Cromwell ruled in his place.

Cromwell was a Puritan – a person with strict religious beliefs, and he thought that fun and entertainment were bad. Cromwell's government closed down theatres, and some of the buildings were destroyed.

New theatre buildings

In 1660 Parliament decided to have a king again. Restoring (bringing back) the king was called the Restoration. Under the new king, Charles II, theatres reopened and new ones were built.

The Sheldonian Theatre in Oxford opened in 1669. It was different from the old theatres like the Rose. It was more like a modern theatre, with everything under one big roof.

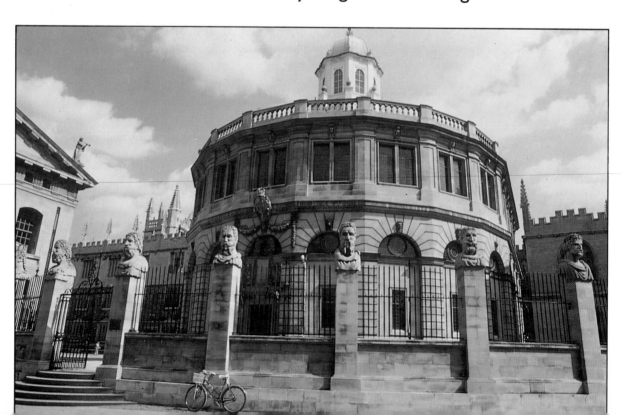

The Sheldonian Theatre, Oxford, as it is today.

A portrait of Aphra Behn.

Cheeky plays

Aphra Behn wrote plays for Restoration theatres. She led a very interesting life, which gave her ideas for her plays. She lived abroad for several years and she worked as a spy for King Charles II. Some of her plays were full of fun and naughtiness. Theatre audiences were pleased to see lively plays again after putting up with Cromwell's strict rules. Women were now allowed to act, but Aphra Behn was the only woman who wrote successful plays in Tudor and Stuart times. Can you think of a possible reason for this?

Samuel Pepys

Samuel Pepys was a wealthy man who lived in London at the time of the Restoration. He kept a diary from 1660 to 1669. In it he wrote about life in London when Charles II was king. He described how a dreadful disease called the plague struck London in 1665. He also wrote about the fire that destroyed more than half the city in 1666.

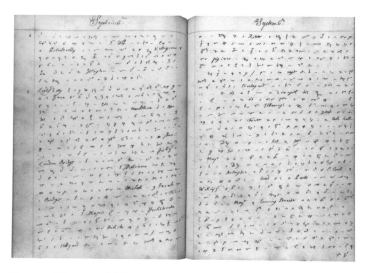

Part of Pepys' *Diary*.

A secret code

Pepys wrote his diary in a sort of code, so you probably won't be able to read the page above. Some of the things he put in his diary were cheeky and rude and he wanted to keep them secret from everyone!

Pepys the musician

Pepys was good at all sorts of things, including music. The picture on the left shows him holding a piece of music that he had written.

A portrait of Samuel Pepys with his music.

The Great Plague of 1665

During the plague, Pepys saw dozens of bodies being heaped on carts to be buried in huge pits. He also saw houses with prayers and red crosses painted on the doors. The people who lived in the houses had the plague and were warning their friends to stay away in case they caught it.

One day, when Pepys was riding in a horse-drawn coach, the driver went half-blind because he had caught the plague. He staggered down into the road, unable to drive any further.

The fire

The Fire of London upset Pepys even more than the plague. He wrote:

> " *It made me weep to see it, the churches, houses all on fire and flaming at once; and a horrid noise the flames made and the cracking of houses at their ruin.* "

A painting showing the Fire of London in 1666. You can see people escaping from the fire in boats.

1628
William Harvey proves that blood goes round the body.

1660–69
Samuel Pepys writes his Diary.

1665
Nearly 50,000 people in London die from the plague.

1666
The Fire of London.

1670–89
Aphra Behn writes her plays.

Sir Christopher Wren

After the fire of 1666 many of London's buildings and streets had to be rebuilt, and this gave a man called Christopher Wren the chance to show his skill as an architect (a designer of buildings).

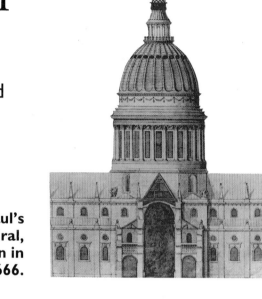

St Paul's Cathedral, drawn in 1666.

This picture shows **Sir Christopher Wren. How does it tell you that Wren was an architect? How does it show that he worked in London?**

Rebuilding the city

The fire had spread easily because London had very narrow streets and most of the buildings were made of wood.

Christopher Wren planned a new city, with open spaces, wide streets and buildings made of brick and stone. Some parts of London were rebuilt according to Wren's new plans. They were cleaner and healthier than before. London has never had another serious outbreak of plague and there were no more fires like the one in 1666.

Wren's monument

St Paul's Cathedral in London is the most famous building Wren designed. After his death Wren was buried there. The Latin words on his tombstone say, 'If you want to see Wren's monument look all around' – in other words, look at his magnificent cathedral.

The Royal Society

Wren and Pepys were both interested in science. They were glad when King Charles II helped to form a new society called the Royal Society for the Promotion of Natural Knowledge, in 1662. The Royal Society still exists today, and it helps scientists with their work. Pepys went to one of its first meetings, and he wrote about what he saw in his diary:

The inside of St Paul's Cathedral today.

> " *There was a pretty experiment of the blood of one dog let out into the body of another, while all his own ran out. The first died on the spot, and the other is very well and likely to do well. This may be of mighty use to men's health, for the mending of bad blood by the borrowing from a better body.* "

Pepys was right: modern doctors use the idea, called blood transfusion, to treat their patients.

Pepys felt that science was for men, not women, and he was very annoyed when a wealthy woman called Margaret Cavendish joined the Royal Society in 1667. She did a lot to encourage science, but some unkind men called her 'Mad Madge' and no more women were allowed to join the society for nearly three hundred years.

New progress in science

In Stuart times people began to use lenses to find out more about the world. A lens makes things look bigger, and we sometimes call it a magnifying glass. Scientists learned to make telescopes and microscopes by using two or three lenses together. These new instruments helped them to look at far-away things like stars and planets, and tiny things like insects and germs.

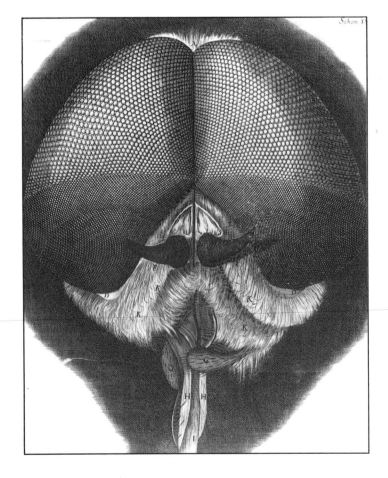

(Right) Hooke's microscope, which was about 60 cm high.

(Left) Hooke's drawing of a fly's head, as seen through his microscope.

A fly's eye

Robert Hooke was one of the first people to use a microscope for careful scientific work. The top part of the drawing on the left looks like the scales on a fish, but it really shows the tiny parts of a fly's eye.

Rainbow colours

Lenses work by bending light. A scientist called Isaac Newton studied light carefully. He used glass prisms to show that white light is made up of all the colours in the rainbow.

Gravity

Newton studied gravity (the invisible way things pull on each other). This led him to work out why the planets move through space in the way they do.

Below is a pound note from the 1980s, showing Newton and one of his telescopes. The oval shapes are the paths planets follow as they go round the sun.

1660–85
Sir Christopher Wren designs many new buildings.

1660–85
Robert Hooke and Isaac Newton study light and gravity.

1662
The Royal Society is officially formed.

27

Timeline

1480	1500	1520	1540	1560	1580

Tudors

1485 HENRY VII

1509 HENRY VIII

1547 EDWARD VI

1553 MARY TUDOR

1558 ELIZABETH I

1480–1500	1500–1520	1520–1540	1540–1560	1560–1580	1580–1600
1492 Columbus sails to America.	**1500–1547** Sheep farmers enclose common land. **1509** Cabot tries to sail round the north of Canada.	**1520** The Spaniards begin to settle on the American mainland. **1534** Henry VIII becomes Head of the Church in England and Wales. **1536** Henry VIII's second wife, Anne Boleyn, is put to death. **1539** Henry VIII has the monasteries destroyed.	**1543** Andreas Vesalius publishes his book about the human body. **1545** The *Mary Rose* sinks. **1547–1553** Many schools and colleges are built. **1549** Robert Kett leads a rebellion in Norfolk. **1553–1558** Many Protestants are put to death.	**1567** As a Catholic, Mary Queen of Scots flees from Scotland but is imprisoned in England. **1577** Sir Francis Drake sets off on his voyage around the world.	**1587** Mary Queen of Scots is executed. **1588** The Spanish Armada is defeated. **1595** Sir Walter Raleigh explores South America. **1590–1616** William Shakespeare writes his plays.

1600   1620   1640   1660   1680   1700

Stuarts

1603 JAMES I (JAMES VI OF SCOTLAND)

1625 CHARLES I

1649–1660 COMMONWEALTH
1653 OLIVER CROMWELL
1658 RICHARD CROMWELL
1660 CHARLES II

1685 JAMES II
1688 WILLIAM III & MARY II

1702–1714 ANNE

1600–1620	1620–1640	1640–1660	1660–1680	1680–1700	1700–1710
1605 The Gunpowder Plot.	**1628** William Harvey describes how blood goes round the body.	**1642** The Civil War begins.	**1665** The plague kills 50,000 people in London.	**1690** The Battle of the Boyne.	**1707** England and Scotland are officially united.
1607 Henry Hudson sets off to explore the coast of northern Canada.	**1630–1641** Charles I rules without Parliament.	**1646** Charles I is captured and imprisoned.	**1666** The Fire of London.	**1694** Queen Mary dies.	
1610 Hudson discovers a huge bay in northern Canada. It is called Hudson Bay.		**1649** Charles I is executed.	**1670** The Hudson Bay Company is founded.	**1680–1695** Henry Purcell writes his music.	
1620 The Pilgrim Fathers settle in America.		**1649–1660** England, Wales and Scotland are ruled without a king or queen.	**1660–1669** Samuel Pepys writes his diary.		
			1660–1685 Hooke and Newton study light and gravitation. Sir Christopher Wren designs many new buildings.		
			1670–1689 Aphra Behn writes her lively plays.		

Glossary

Archaeologists People who study the past from remains.

Circulation The movement of blood around the body.

Compass An instrument with a magnetic needle, which people use to find their way.

Inn A small hotel, often used by travellers.

Lens A piece of glass or other material with one or more curved surfaces, used to make objects look larger.

Parliament The building where a group of people meet to work out the laws for their country.

Plague A serious disease that humans can catch from rats, and which spreads very easily.

Prism A specially-shaped piece of glass used for breaking light down into the colours of the rainbow.

Puritan A religious Christian, (especially one from Stuart times) who believes in living and praying in a simple way.

Restoration Parliament's decision in 1660 to having a king again.

Scholar A learned person who spends his or her time studying.

Tombstone A stone to mark a person's grave.

Books to read

Carter, M., Culpin, C. & Kinloch, N. *Past into Present 2: 1400–1700* (Collins Educational, 1990)

Martin, C. *Shakespeare* (Wayland, 1988)

McTavish, D. *Isaac Newton* (Wayland, 1990)

Middleton, H. *Everyday Life in the Sixteenth Century* (Macdonald, 1982)

Triggs, T.D. *Tudor Britain* (Wayland, 1989)

Triggs, T.D. *Tudor and Stuart Times* (Folens, 1992)

Wood, T. *The Stuarts* (Ladybird, 1991)

Places to visit

The Museum of London,
London
The Science Museum,
London
Shakespeare's birthplace,
Stratford-on-Avon, Warwickshire
St Paul's Cathedral,
London
Oxford
Go to see the colleges and other buildings.

Write to Historic Scotland, Education Dept, 20 Brandon St, Edinburgh EH3 5RA for details of free educational visits in Scotland.

Index

Words printed in **bold** are subjects that appear in pictures as well as in the text.